MW01601628

Instructor's Manual to Accompany

Beyond Feelings
A Guide to Critical Thinking

FIFTH EDITION

Vincent Ryan Ruggiero

Mayfield Publishing Company
Mountain View, California
London • Toronto

International Standard Book Number: 1-55934-981-6

Manufactured in the United States of America

Mayfield Publishing Company
1280 Villa Street
Mountain View, CA 94041

Contents

Preface   v

Part I: The Context   1

Chapter 1: Who Are You?   1

Chapter 2: What Is Critical Thinking?   2

Chapter 3: What Is Truth?   3

Chapter 4: What Does It Mean To Know?   5

Chapter 5: How Good Are Your Opinions?   5

Part II: The Problems   8

Chapter 6: The Basic Problem: "Mine Is Better"   8

Chapter 7: Resistance to Change   8

Chapter 8: Conformity   9

Chapter 9: Face Saving   10

Chapter 10: Stereotyping   11

Chapter 11: Oversimplification   11

Chapter 12: Hasty Conclusion   14

Chapter 13: Unwarranted Assumption   13

Chapter 14: Logical Fallacies   14

Chapter 15: The Problems in Combination   16

Part III: A Strategy   19

Chapter 16: Knowing Yourself   19

Chapter 17: Being Observant   20

Chapters 18–20: Clarifying Issues, Conducting Inquiry,
    Forming a Judgment   21

iii

Preface

The purpose of *Beyond Feelings* is to introduce students to the process of critical thinking and guide them to develop confidence and skill in applying that process to issues. The measure of students' success will not be how closely their responses match the "official" answers. Rather, it will be the quality of their analysis, writing, and discussion. This is not to say that all answers are equal or that the substance of students' responses is unimportant. Far from it. It is only to say that the answers should be determined by the evidence and reasoning that supports them and not be handed down by the author or the instructor. Accordingly, this manual does not serve as an "answer key." Instead, it discusses difficulties students may experience in doing the assignments and provides suggestions for overcoming those difficulties. For applications in which no difficulties are expected, no comments are made.

Managing the "Thinking Classroom"

Not everyone who adopts this book for his or her classes will need assistance in managing thinking instruction. Many of you have used critical thinking textbooks for years. (Indeed, some professors have told me they have used this book since it was first published in 1975.) This section is designed for instructors who have little or no experience teaching thinking skills.

The teaching methods that work effectively for imparting information are seldom appropriate for developing students' thinking skills and habits. Following are some approaches that have proven effective in the "thinking classroom."

Minimize lecturing—it tends to reinforce passivity in students.

Avoid one-on-one exchanges with students. Encourage students to discuss ideas with one another.

Quit being the "answer person." Redirect students' questions to other students.

Avoid assigning issues on which you have taken an irrevocable position. You'll have difficulty being fair-minded about them.

Ask fewer questions that demand simple recall and more that require students to evaluate existing ideas or generate new ones.

Since thoughtful responses take time to fashion, remain silent for at least ten or fifteen seconds after asking any question calling for thought.

Disguise your reactions to student responses so that they will weigh ideas and not just "read" you.

Encourage students to think in terms of cases and scenarios that test opinions, and not just in terms of assertions.

Require students to support their assertions with evidence.

Guide students to defer judgment until they have considered many possibilities.

Keep your interventions in student discussion infrequent and brief.

Be sensitive to students' need for encouragement. Give approval for worthy efforts, even flawed or unfruitful ones.

Gradually reduce the level of your assistance, giving a lot at the outset of the course but very little toward the end.

The best way to keep students thinking is to ask them questions. The following questions are among the most effective:

What do you think about this matter?

What line of reasoning led you to that conclusion?

What evidence supports your position?

Can you give an example?

How typical is that example?

In what way does your experience support or challenge the author's idea?

What additional information might help you reach a conclusion? Where might you find that information?

What objections could be raised to your idea?

Are any of these objections wholly or partly valid? Explain.

What other views of this issue are possible? Which of those is most reasonable?

Part I: The Context

This section introduces students to key cognitive concepts—individuality, critical thinking, truth, knowledge, and opinion—and attempts to dispel ideas that hinder the effective use of their minds.

Chapter 1: Who Are You?

The idea that we are influenced by other people and by the culture we live in is not particularly pleasant. Nor is the related idea that we are not as individualistic as we have always thought. If students tend to resist these ideas, you may wish to lead discussion in the following direction:

> Do you know any people who are followers rather than leaders, who imitate rather than originate behavior? If so, do any of them acknowledge the fact? What makes them deny what is so obvious to others? Is this tendency to deny unpleasant realities peculiar to those people or a general human tendency? Is such denial admirable?

Applications 1, 2

Students are usually shocked, and sometimes angered, at the realization that their attention has been so blatantly manipulated by the producers of television programs and commercials. They will want to discuss particular findings, specific commercials, and so on. That's fine. But be sure they give adequate consideration to the broad range of possible effects of such manipulation. Among the questions you may wish to introduce are the following: What effects, if any, have several decades of this manipulation had on the political process? What learning problems, if any, are related to a short attention span? Can you think of any ways in which a short attention span could hurt personal relationships and/or performance on the job?

Application 4

Some students may go to the trouble of videotaping what they have seen, so try to allow time for them to show at least a brief sampling of what they found and to share their interpretations of it.

1

Applications 5–7

Having several students read aloud their responses to application 5 will help reinforce the message of the chapter. (Many, perhaps most, students will prefer not to discuss their answers to applications 6 and 7.)

Application 8

If you have assigned all ten statements, you may wish to ask for a show of hands to learn which ones were most fruitful to analyze and limit class discussion to those.

Group Discussion Exercise

The purpose of this exercise, in this and subsequent chapters, is to extend students' growing confidence and skill in *individual* analysis of issues to *group* analysis of issues. The special challenge in group work, of course, is to be both cooperative and responsibly assertive.

Chapter 2: What Is Critical Thinking?

Because this chapter is especially important in laying the foundation for critical thinking, you may wish to allow more time than usual for discussing its contents, perhaps incorporating the first four applications in that discussion. Encourage students to identify parts of the chapter that they do not understand or are uncertain about. Invite them to share with the class their self-analyses in the first four applications. These are not likely to be as private as those in Chapter 1, and everyone will be heartened to learn that others have had similar experiences and have weaknesses as well as strengths.

Application 5

Among the many questions students may ask are these: (a) Is it reasonable to expect *war* reporting to avoid such pictures? (b) Is delayed dating in any way beneficial? (c) Isn't it possible that he didn't see you, perhaps because he was preoccupied with a problem or concern? (d) What percentage of the news is so important to viewers that it won't "keep" for six or eight hours? (e) Will any students feel uncomfortable having to recite a prayer of a religion they do not believe in?

Application 7

Students' analyses will be incomplete unless they recognize and evaluate these hidden premises: (a) There is some connection between the dealer's selecting quality cars and the customer's ability/willingness to make payments. (b) More nurturing is better than less. (c) The term *family* is applicable to any situation in which love exists. (d) The government is the only agency that is capable of dealing with the problem. (You may wish to remind students that an argument is not necessarily unsound because it contains a hidden premise.)

Applications 8, 9

In evaluating students' analyses and guiding discussion, keep the emphasis on the quality of the evidence and reasoning offered in support of students' views.

Chapter 3: What Is Truth?

Application 2

If one starts with the belief that individuals create their own truth, one might be motivated to analyze what led Comte, Spencer, and Marx to their "truths" but not to which of them, if any, best fits reality. One's relativistic premise would have rendered that question irrelevant.

Application 3

a. The hidden premise is "The only relevant consideration in dating is whether the individuals are unmarried adults." This premise is flawed. Another relevant consideration is whether their dating would in any way violate a preexisting obligation. It could be argued that the professor's obligation to grade students fairly, based solely on their individual achievement, would be at least compromised.

b. The first premise is accurate as stated, but incomplete. In addition to violating the law, copying violates a contract the student entered into freely. (Software labels clearly indicate that opening the package and using the software constitutes acceptance of the copyright terms.) So the student is breaking both the law and his or her own promise. The fact that copying is commonplace may make students *feel* strongly that it is acceptable. This provides a good opportunity to remind students that the name of the book, *Beyond Feelings*, is also an important goal of critical thinking.

c. The flaw lies in the conclusion. That "equality is a myth" does not follow logically from the premises. What does follow is that complete equality does not yet exist. Discussion should examine the meaning of "all men are created equal." Does it refer to the physical or the metaphysical? Does it describe a real condition or an ideal one, something to take for granted or to strive to accomplish?

Applications 4–6

The more slowly and methodically discussion proceeds, question by question, the more effectively these applications will work to reinforce the lessons of the chapter.

Application 7

a. The central question is whether Martha or anyone else has the "right to classify what exists in someone else's uterus." By challenging that right, Marian is implying that a four-month fetus in one uterus could be human whereas a four-month fetus in another uterus might not be human. That implication cannot be taken for granted, but should be tested for reasonableness.

b. The key questions are as follows: What evidence, if any, suggests that suicide attempts increase after television shows "about suicide" are aired? Does that evidence apply to all shows "about suicide," only to dramatizations, or more narrowly still, to dramatizations that suggest approval of suicide? Is the evidence strong enough to suggest *causation?*

c. In order to decide this one, students will have to determine what standards of investigation characterize science—for example, replicability and falsifiability—and whether those standards are operative in astrology.

d. Rocky's final assertion should be checked out against the chapters specified. Did the author say what Rocky asserts or something different?

Application 8

Student discussion should reinforce the chapter's message about truth.

Chapter 4: What Does It Mean To Know?

Application 1

a. This argument contains an unstated premise— that displeasing the majority is the only possible reason for abridging the free exercise of religion. This is not so, as the prohibition of the Mormon practice of polygamy made clear. In this case, cruelty to animals is another possible reason.

b. The second premise is open to question. Generally speaking, of course, speech is protected by the Constitution. But one classic exception is the prohibition of falsely shouting "Fire!" in a crowded public place. Another exception is making harassing statements to others. An interesting question in this case is, Is panhandling a form of harassment?

Application 2

It reinforces, of course. The effort to explain exactly how it does will reinforce the chapter's message for students.

Application 3

The average person's knowledge about most subjects comes from journalism, as opposed to, say, scholarly books. Any tendency to unreliability will thus diminish the quality of the average person's knowledge. An interesting question for students to ponder is, What precautions can people take to maintain or increase the quality of their knowledge?

Application 4

If students have trouble with these scenarios, have them consider whether *assume, guess,* or *prefer to believe* fit the circumstances better than the word *know.* They should also consider whether the reason for believing is sufficient.

Chapter 5: How Good Are Your Opinions?

Application 1

If students harbor the impression that magazines have no editorial slant, their first reaction to all four descriptions will probably be shock. That reaction may be enough for some to form the opinion that all four magazines should be excluded from the library collection. Further, conservatives may wish to exclude *The Nation;* liberals, *Human Events;* religious believers, *Free Inquiry;* and heterosexuals, *Paidika.* Discussion should help them see that neither ignorance of the reality of editorial bias nor personal preference is a legitimate basis for excluding them. Enterprising students will no doubt check *Magazines for Libraries* to see if more objective alternatives to these magazines are available. If they are, one might reasonably (though perhaps not compellingly) argue for excluding these. Note that the dual purpose of *Paidika* makes judgment more difficult. One might reasonably say, "Its academic purpose makes it acceptable, but its other purpose gives me pause. If its treatment of the illegal activity of pedophilia is partisan rather than purely academic, I oppose its inclusion."

Application 5

The answer, of course, is (b). Statements of preference are of little relevance to critical thinking because they are matters of taste rather than judgment.

Application 6

The answer is all of them except (c).

Application 7

a. The hidden premise is "No other country or group of countries could pose a serious threat to U.S. security." It could be argued that the Soviet threat consisted primarily of their stockpile of weapons. An interesting question is, Where did all the weapons go that used to belong to the Soviet Union? If they were retained by individual Soviet republics (a notable example being Russia), or sold to other countries such as Iran or Iraq, then the threat could be as great or, given the lack of central control, even greater than before.

b. The hidden premise is that responsibility and hard work are important values that should not be lost. Perhaps the key question to be considered is, Does the present welfare system cause people to lose self-respect and confidence and make them dependent?

c. The hidden premise is that embarrassing and humiliating experiences have no positive value for students.

Application 12

Students may get caught up in the heat of this dialogue. For example, some may share Henrietta's anger about what she sees as male hypocrisy; others may resent that anger. Some may see distasteful sarcasm in Burt's remarks, whereas others may see them as playful teasing. Be sure students don't get so focused on these matters that they fail to address the issue of alleged discrimination.

Part II: The Problems

This section addresses the most common logical fallacies that undermine thinking and suggests how students can avoid them in their own thinking and detect them in the thinking of others.

Chapter 6: The Basic Problem: "Mine Is Better"

Application 5

a. The assumption behind this argument is that the benefits cited— so-called character building and the expression of school spirit and loyalty—deserve the same priority as the acquisition of an education. This argument is likely to generate vigorous discussion, as well it should.

b. The leap from the first premise to the second is large. The assumption seems to be that distributing birth control devices is an educational service. Discussion should address, among other considerations, the logic by which the traditional role of educa-tion— —developing understanding and intellectual skills—was broadened to cover medical services.

Application 7

a. The central issue is Bernice's contention that loving someone entails sparing the person embarrassment. Before having students discuss their responses to this dialogue in class, consider having them list, perhaps on the blackboard, contrary views of the requirements of love, and then decide whether any are better than Bernice's.

b. Consider adding to the discussion the question, Would you take the same view if the teacher taught, say, second grade?

Chapter 7: Resistance to Change

Application 1

a. Discussion should address these questions, among others: Is the "clogging" a serious enough problem to warrant removing the law books? Would another remedy be more reasonable and effective? Does the availability of law books in prison really *encourage* the filing of lawsuits or merely enable prisoners to do the research necessary for filing?

b. The hidden premise is that a three-member presidential "board" would be able to handle the work of the office more effectively and efficiently. Students should consider whether having three presidents would create new and perhaps more difficult problems than the present ones.

Application 3

One useful way to start discussion of this exercise is to ask which of the ideas, (a) through (k), were most interesting and revealing of resistance to change. Focusing on a fewer number will allow for greater depth of discussion. The range of responses will undoubtedly include some that are irrational—"I've never heard that before, so I'm against it"—and others that, though almost instantly arrived at, have some basis in reason. The main lesson students should take from this assignment is that resistance to change is not so much objectionable in itself as objectionable in its tendency to short-circuit critical thinking.

Application 5

Whichever side of this censorship issue students come down on, they should appreciate that *neither* Georgina's nor Ernest's argument is *totally* without merit.

Chapter 8: Conformity

Application 5

The argument looks nice and tight. The problem is not so much in what it says as in what it ignores—the rights of nonsmokers. The question is in what circumstances, if any, smokers' rights ought to take precedence; and in what circumstances, if any, nonsmokers' rights should.

Chapter 9: Face Saving

Application 1

All the statements are compatible with what is said in the chapter.

Application 2

On the face of it, Seneca's observation seems silly because it is counterintuitive. However, on reflection students should be able to see that it is a genuine insight. Every time we deal with someone we have offended, we are reminded of our offense. In time, the tendency to save face can prompt us to regard that reminder as itself offensive *and the innocent person as guilty of the offense.* Interestingly, the act of apologizing when we have offended others lessens the chance that this reaction will occur.

Application 6

One explanation is that Sherry felt guilty that she has not told her parents that she is living with her boyfriend and has spent their money on him without their permission. Further, her desire to save face caused her to seek a confrontation so that she could retroactively justify her behavior and remove her guilt.

Application 7

Students should see, among other things, that the issue of what should be done with the man who took advantage of the woman is a separate issue from whether abortion is justified in this case. They should also realize that this case is so unusual that it constitutes a rare exception. Thus one could concede that abortion is appropriate in this case and still hold that it is wrong in the majority of cases.

Application 10

Some relevant questions: Would Quentin's approach give children the impression that their parents had no views on such matters as religion and politics, or that they held those matters to be of little importance? Who else, besides parents, share their views with children? Teachers, other children and adults, spokespeople for popular culture such as rock music stars and actors, and authors of the literature children read and the movies they view. Would the child benefit by being exposed to these influences but not the influence of parents?

Chapter 10: Stereotyping

Application 1

a. The hidden premise is that zoos take animals from the wild and exhibit them for human pleasure. Discussion should focus on exactly what the phrase "natural rights" means in relation to animals. Do they have the same rights as people? Where do they get such rights? (For example, are rabbits, squirrels, and rattlesnakes "endowed by their Creator with certain inalienable rights"?) People who argue that animals have such rights sometimes imply that their opponents approve the misuse of animals. However, the traditional view of the relationship between humans and animals holds that humans are the stewards of all living things, a serious responsibility.

Application 6

a. Cecil's final comment reveals that he is stereotyping all religious people as fundamentalists who interpret the Bible literally. In reality, not all religious people are fundamentalists. But speaking of interpreting the Bible literally, Jesus said to the wealthy man in Matthew 19:21—"If you wish to be complete, go and sell your possessions and *give to the poor,* and you shall have treasure in heaven; and come, follow Me." (Emphasis added.) Not only did both Cecil and the Texas businessman fail to take that advice literally; they ignored it altogether! Be sure to point out this inconsistency to students and explain that contradicting one's own stated principles can be devastating to one's argument.

b. Renee clearly stereotypes transsexuals, but Christine's argument that a sex-change operation is of no significance is open to question. Of course, one could argue that it is significant but not sufficient reason for firing the officer.

Chapter 11: Oversimplification

Application 1

Any of the six choices could qualify as a cause of oversimplification in a given instance.

Application 2

Some interesting questions that class discussion should address: Did the Founding Fathers consider the United States "under God"? Where did the phrase "separation of church and state" originate? What was it designed to prevent?

Application 3

a. Question: Judging from this quotation, what would Rousseau say about the expression "moral reasoning" or "thinking critically about moral issues"?

b. If students have difficulty with this one, have them identify a number of specific situations demanding moral choice and then ask whether elected officials should meet a higher standard in those situations.

c. The key to their making a thoughtful decision about this one is to understand that when someone is killed with a gun, the gun and the killer have different functions. The gun is the instrument and the killer is the agent.

Chapter 12: Hasty Conclusion

Application 1

Some students may select the most modest of the choices proposed: "Susan behaved rudely." However, the evidence is insufficient to support even that conclusion, let alone the more extravagant ones. Susan may simply not have recognized Louise.

Application 2

Students may be tempted to jump to the conclusion that Cuba's policy is outrageous. The fact that Cuba is a communist country not on good terms with the United States may reinforce that temptation. But before making that leap, they should consider Cuba's policy dispassionately. You may want to explain that the practice of quarantining people suffering from highly contagious diseases was widespread in the United States up until about fifty years ago. The reason was similar to the present situation in Cuba—medical science was not able to control the spread of the diseases or inoculate people against them. (This is not to say, of course, that Cuba's policy is the right one.)

Application 3–7

Students may feel more comfortable exchanging assertions than presenting and evaluating the evidence on which the assertions are based. If that is the case, you will have to monitor the discussion closely and redirect their focus to the evidence whenever they stray from it. At the beginning of the discussion of each application, you may wish to have a student come to the blackboard and write down all the evidence members of the class accumulated. This approach will help students who had too little evidence understand their shortcomings. Remarks such as the following will also help guide discussion:

> "You've made your point quite clearly, Mary. Now explain the thinking that led you to that conclusion."

> "Tell us, Charles, what information you obtained before judging this case. Is there any item of evidence on the board that you did not have and that would have led you to modify your conclusion?"

Chapter 13: Unwarranted Assumption

Application 1

The main assumptions are (a) that force that does not produce fear of serious injury or death is less objectionable, or even acceptable; (b) that in rape, unlike in burglaries, carjackings, and other crimes, saying "stop that" has no legal force; (c) that rape is usually, or at least often, committed in public.

Application 2

The assumption was that automobiles would always be chauffeur-driven.

Application 3

Key questions to be addressed include the following: What part or parts of the Constitution do the *opponents* of school prayer cite in support of their position? Which interpretation of those parts is most reasonable, that of the opponents or that of the proponents of school prayer?

Application 4

a. The assumption is that money is the only issue that could be involved in the strike.

b. The assumption in this dialogue takes either of two forms. The specific form is that a film about lesbians cannot be a quality film. The general form is that the subject matter of a film (as opposed to cinematic treatment of that subject) alone determines the film's quality.

c. The assumption is that the amount of time one spends in preparation for an examination should govern the grade one receives. The investment of a great deal of time, in other words, should guarantee a good grade.

d. The assumption is that what one hears in the supermarket must be true. (This is related to the assumption that what one reads in supermarket tabloids must be true.)

Chapter 14: Logical Fallacies

Application 2

a. The hidden premise in this argument is "For a professor to use a book he himself wrote and gets royalties from is improper." Many students will be unfamiliar with the circumstances under which textbooks are usually written: A professor finds that existing textbooks don't provide the course material he or she wants students to have and so invests the time (usually several years) and effort to create a book that does. According to the argument in question, the professor should then be required to adopt one of the books he or she found wanting in the first place. [For the record, in thirty years of teaching, I never heard a student make this statement or advance the related argument. However, a respected judge in New York State once expressed it to me in a cocktail party conversation, adding that he had always resented being required to buy a textbook written by his law school professor. I inferred that the subject in question was not logic.]

b. Important questions: Is gambling addictive in the same way that, say, smoking or drinking alcohol are, or only metaphorically so? To what extent are gamblers responsible for their behavior?

c. The hidden premise is that such clogging and burdening is unfair.

d. Students should recognize that the conclusion in this argument is expressed in the first sentence. They should address the following questions: Is it true that every voter's ballot is canceled by another voter's ballot? (If this were so, then every election would be either undecided or decided by an odd ballot.) Is the "robbing" propensity precisely equal in all politicians? (If not, then it does matter who gets elected.)

e. Key questions include the following: Is dogfighting properly classified as a sport? Is a dog merely property? Should the "owner" of a living creature be able to do with it whatever he or she wishes? Students should note the extravagance of the word "whatever" in this argument.

f. The issue in this argument continues to generate a great deal of heat, perhaps more heat than light. Fruitful lines of thought and discussion include the following: The term "old system" is vague—does the argument call for returning to the system that discriminated against minorities, or to the practice of hiring people according to their credentials only? In what specific ways does affirmative action discriminate against "the majority"? How often do those ways occur? Often enough to say that affirmative action does more harm than good?

g. Interesting question: Will this practice help American workers and their companies improve and become more competitive?

h. Not entirely silly question: Why can't the ticket be one-way?

i. This argument has no premises. It consists merely of a double conclusion. However, the implication seems to be that all soldiers need the same physical strength required for feats of athleticism and hand-to-hand combat. The reasonableness of this notion can be determined by considering the specific demands of the various jobs in the modern military.

j. Students may be inclined to deal with this argument in all-or-nothing fashion. It will be more prudent to test each of the categories individually and decide the issue of fitness accordingly.

k. Key questions: Keeping in mind how easy it is to make an accusation, is it fair to place such a burden on accused people? How does one go about proving one didn't do something? (One way would be to prove that someone else did it, which would be to assign defendants the role of police investigators. How reasonable is such an assignment?)

l. The hidden premise is that it is unfair to set a more demanding standard (regarding gambling) for those who participate in sports than for spectators. Is it unfair or is there a good reason for setting a higher standard?

m. Some important questions: Have college courses been "watered down"? Has the college degree been "rendered meaningless"? In all fields or merely some? If some, which ones? If college were reserved for those who excelled in a demanding high school program, what percentage of high school graduates would qualify for college? What would happen to colleges in this case? What would happen to the students who didn't qualify?

Chapter 15: The Problems in Combination

Application 1

a. The hidden premise is that realistic presentations are more appropriate or desirable than their opposite. But what exactly is their opposite? If it is *unrealistic,* then the hidden premise seems reasonable enough. But if the opposite of realistic is *idealistic,* the premise is open to question. Discussion should also cover these questions: How realistic are contemporary shows? Does canned laughter resound every five seconds in real life? Is sexual passion the exclusive preoccupation of the unmarried in real life? Does one hair-raising, breathtaking, exhilarating experience follow another in rapid succession in real life? Are people in real life free of the need to sleep or go to the bathroom, as their reel counterparts appear to be? Is it reasonable or responsible to continue questionable programming practices until they are *proven* harmful? (In other words, would a lesser standard than proof, such as probability, be more appropriate?)

b. This argument asserts that hate crimes do more emotional harm than other crimes. Does any evidence exist to support this contention? (Incidentally, what is the opposite of a hate crime? A *love* crime? This is not as silly as it sounds. It could be argued that every crime is, in a real sense, a hate crime.) The old legal proverb suggests that the punishment should fit the crime. Does this new standard for hate crimes make the punishment fit, instead, the mental state of the victim? Is it not conceivable that some victims of non-hate crimes are more emotionally fragile than some victims of hate crimes and therefore are more deeply affected by their victimization? In such cases, should the perpetrators who victimized them suffer a greater penalty for that reason? Most important, how exactly will the level of emotional harm to specific victims be determined?

Application 2

a. The most significant errors in thinking, in the order of their appearance, are as follows. *Oversimplification* in the idea that lesbianism is willful moral degeneracy. (Despite where one stands on the issue of whether homosexuality is "natural," to suggest it is *freely chosen as degenerative behavior* is a distortion of the complex and, as yet, not fully understood reality.) *Stereotyping* in both Ann's and Dan's finger-pointing explanations of why their daughter is a lesbian. *Unwarranted assumption* in their statement about dorm crowding—the specific assumption is that crowding creates lesbians. (By this logic, dorms that assign every student to a private room will as a result have only heterosexual students.) *Hasty conclusion* in their holding the dean of students responsible for the number of students in the dormitory. (He or she may not be.)

b. Stephen's first error ("what better break . . .") is to invoke the *stereotype* of Jews as quick to take care of their own. (This could be alternatively classified as the *unwarranted assumption* that Mr. Stein will give Stephen special treatment because both are Jewish.) Simultaneously, Stephen assumes without warrant that Mr. Stein is Jewish. Many people named Stein are not Jewish. These errors lead him to ignore the signal implicit in his midterm grade and set him up for failure. His postfailure behavior is a form of *face-saving*.

Application 3

The principal problems illustrated in this case are face-saving and conformity. The audience began by assuming that the talk would be meaningful. Given the occasion, the impressive "credentials" of the speaker, and the scholarly sounding title, this assumption was warranted. However, once he began to speak, the assumption should have given way to a preliminary assessment based on the substance of his remarks. The only reasonable and honest response to double-talk would have been "I don't understand this" or, more confidently, "This is nonsense." But fear of losing face with their peers overpowered good sense and honesty alike. No doubt they wondered, "What if I say 'This is nonsense' and others say 'No, it makes perfect sense to us'?" So they did as they learned to do in undergraduate and graduate school when they didn't understand something—nodded their heads in agreement and made believe they were impressed. When they looked around and saw others doing the same thing, the urge to conform reinforced the urge to save face. Later, when asked for their reaction, what else could they do but praise the speaker.

Applications 4–6

Before having students share their responses to these applications with one another and debating the issues, have them explain how they went about checking for errors in their own thinking and what they found. This may be awkward for many students because they have little experience in applying critical thinking to their own thinking and even less experience in talking about this process. Stress that finding their own tendencies to error and/or actual errors is an *accomplishment* that demonstrates their progress in thinking. (They may be inclined to regard it as something to be ashamed of.) Everyone will profit from hearing how others found and overcame their problems in thinking. This approach to class discussion will also help students prepare for the more comprehensive self-examination they will undertake in the Chapter 16 applications.

Part III: A Strategy

This section offers a cumulative strategy for dealing with issues, each chapter presenting a particular step. Some of the applications are cumulative, as well.

Chapter 16: Knowing Yourself

Application 1

This application directs students to discuss the findings of their self-analysis. Because students may feel awkward about sharing their findings with classmates, this discussion is perhaps best limited to the written homework.

Application 2

a. The hidden premise is that children's actions are necessarily in keeping with their upbringing; in other words, they never act contrary to what their parents taught them. If this premise is false, then according to the idea in this argument parents will be held responsible for matters over which they lack control.

b. This argument is similar to the *animal* rights argument addressed in an earlier chapter. Among the questions that discussion should cover are the following: What evidence is there that the concept of rights has any application to nonsentient, inanimate matter? Should the corollary of rights—responsibilities—apply to the environment as well? How exactly would this work in, say, the case of ocean waves destroying beachfront houses or a swollen river overflowing it banks and flooding bordering communities? Would the ocean or river be held accountable?

Applications 3, 4

In class discussion of these applications, have students use the same approach they used in the later applications of the previous chapter. In other words, before having them debate the issues, have them explain how they went about checking for errors in their own thinking and what they found.

Chapter 17: Being Observant

Applications 1–5

The importance of observation in critical thinking is difficult to overstate. These applications are designed to underscore this fact and provide students a chance to develop observational skills, but they are also fun to do. (Only the truly daring will attempt application 3, but they are usually rewarded with significant insights into the way one's appearance can affect other people's behavior.)

Application 7

a. The hidden premise is that having a right and being sophisticated are all that is necessary to merit being regarded as an adult under the law. Among the questions class discussion should cover are these: Should level of maturity figure in the equation as well? Does this issue concern a right, as the argument maintains, or a *privilege?* Are young people today really more sophisticated than in any earlier generation in this century?

b. Among the questions that class discussion should address is this: If infertile couples can be given no legal assurance that the contract will be honored, should such contracts be outlawed by the courts?

Applications 8, 9

Begin the discussion of each issue by having students identify their own observations and the observations they solicited from other people. Have someone list the observations on the board as they are stated. Ask these questions about solicited observations:

> From whom did you get those observations? Why did you choose those particular people? (Because they had greater or more specialized expertise or were in an unusually good position to observe?) To what extent did their observations agree with your own? Did any of them challenge yours? In what way, if any, did you modify your viewpoint to reflect the observations that challenged yours?

Next have students consider all the observations listed on the board and decide whether they have changed their minds about the issue during class discussion. Ask those who have changed their minds to explain what specific observations made by others prompted them to revise their view. This class exercise will demonstrate that (a) the more research we do, the surer we can be of our conclusions and (b) changing our minds in light of new evidence is a sign of wisdom rather than weakness.

Chapters 18–20: Clarifying Issues, Conducting Inquiry, Forming a Judgment

To make class discussion of the applications in Chapter 18 more manageable, consider this approach: Ask for a show of hands and determine how many students chose each topic so that you can limit class discussion to the most popular topics. Have two or three students (each for a different topic) go to the board and write the specific subheading they chose to analyze and the questions they raised about it (in other words, their responses to steps 2 and 3 in clarifying an issue).While they are writing, have other members of the class state the subheadings they listed for each of the broad topics represented at the blackboard (step 1 in clarifying an issue). When the students at the board have returned to their seats, discuss each issue; discuss the questions on the blackboard, inviting all students to brainstorm for additional questions.

Before having your students proceed to Chapter 19, do a quick review of the rest of the book, consider whether your course is proceeding ahead of, on, or behind schedule, and decide which of the following approaches will work best for your students.

Fast Approach

(a) Have students read Chapter 19 and do only application 5. (If they wish to change their topic at this point, application 6 provides that option.)

(b) Have students read Chapter 20 and do only application 2.

Slower Approach

(a) Have students read Chapter 19 and do *either* application 1, which offers practice in the process of inquiry, *or* application 2, which offers both that practice plus practice in the valuable skill of summarizing. Then have them do application 5.

(b) Have students read Chapter 20 and do both application 1, which provides further practice in the close analysis of arguments, and application 2.

(c) Have students analyze an issue of their choosing in "Contemporary Issues for Analysis."

Leisurely Approach

(a) Have students read Chapter 19 and do *both* application 1, which offers practice in the process of inquiry, *and* application 2, which offers both that practice plus practice in the valuable skill of summarizing. Then have them do application 5.

(b) Have students read Chapter 20 and do both application 1, which provides further practice in the close analysis of arguments, and application 2.

(c) Have students analyze a number of issues in "Contemporary Issues for Analysis."